Hulu
and Jason Kilar

INTERNET BIOGRAPHIES™

Hulu
and Jason Kilar

LAURA LA BELLA

ROSEN
PUBLISHING®
New York

Published in 2015 by The Rosen Publishing Group, Inc.
29 East 21st Street, New York, NY 10010

Library of Congress Cataloging-in-Publication Data

La Bella, Laura.
Hulu and Jason Kilar/Laura La Bella.
    pages cm.—(Internet biographies)
Includes bibliographical references and index.
ISBN 978-1-4777-7921-7 (library bound)
1. Kilar, Jason, 1971-—Juvenile literature. 2. Telecommunications
engineers—United States—Biography—Juvenile literature.
3. Businesspeople—United States—Biography—Juvenile literature.
4. Hulu—Juvenile literature. 5. Internet television—Juvenile
literature. I. Title.
TK5102.56.K55L325 2015
384.55'8—dc23

                                                    2014008553

Manufactured in the United States of America

Contents

INTRODUCTION

Hulu is one of the most popular online streaming video websites available to consumers. Its goal to help people find and enjoy the world's best video content whenever, wherever, and however they want it has propelled the site to become one of the most popular online content providers and among the easiest to use. While the site was started as a joint venture between NBC Universal and News Corp., which owns the Fox Broadcasting Company, the brains behind the site was its chief executive officer, Jason Kilar.

Kilar, who joined Hulu in 2007, just before the site launched to the public, made it his mission to build Hulu into an easy-to-navigate, online content service that people could easily access from any device. He led the innovation of Hulu's larger video player, pushed content providers to supply television shows and movies in high definition, and spearheaded a new, revolutionary way to stream advertisements within show programming.

Innovation has long been a recurring theme in Kilar's life. His father was an engineer who introduced his family to the personal computer and taught his son computer programming. During Kilar's teen years, he grew obsessed with Walt Disney and the Disney reputation for excellence. He modeled much of his interest in innovation and the customer experience after Walt Disney, who used

Jason Kilar revolutionized television and movie viewing, giving audiences the ability to watch what they wanted to, when and where they chose.

technology to transform animation and the film production process, and revolutionized the hospitality industry. In his college years, first at the University of North Carolina at Chapel Hill and then at Harvard Business School, Kilar had a way of immersing himself in his studies, learning everything he could about business, communications, journalism, and mass media, and applying that knowledge in new ways.

After a short work experience at Disney, Kilar joined Amazon as a product manager before quickly rising in the company's ranks. He pioneered Amazon's DVD business and became a senior vice president for the company. After nearly ten years, Kilar decided to move on from Amazon.

He traveled the world with his family for a year, then got a job offer from Hulu that he couldn't turn down. With a growing trend toward using computers and smartphones for more than just games and communication, and integrating content into these devices, no one had yet developed a successful way to stream television and movie content online. While the idea for Hulu was in place when Kilar started with the company, its growth and momentum were all because of Kilar and his innovative ideas. In the six years he served as chief executive officer for the company, Hulu grew into one of the most popular online venues for television and movie content. Working with studios, television networks, and content creators such as producers and writers, Kilar added to Hulu's library of television shows and movies, and the site began to offer original programming by top directors and producers who were well known in the industry, giving Hulu a level of credibility it didn't have before. Under Kilar's management, Hulu generated nearly $700 million in revenue and generated more than $1 billion in profits for its content providers by 2012.

In 2013, Kilar moved on from Hulu. The company was changing direction, and Kilar decided it was time to explore his own interests. He announced the launch of the Freemont Project, an online content service targeting magazine and newspaper content. The model for this project is similar to his work at Hulu, which transformed the delivery of video content. In Kilar's next venture, he will bring his experiences as an innovative entrepreneur. It's likely that his knowledge of blending traditional and emerging technologies to create new experiences for consumers will transform the print industry next.

CHAPTER 1

Jason Kilar: An Internet Media Visionary

Jason Kilar was born on April 26, 1971, in Murrysville, Pennsylvania, a suburb located about 20 miles (32 kilometers) outside of Pittsburgh. He is one of six children born to Lance and Maureen Kilar. His father was an engineer for Westinghouse Electric Company, a corporation that provides fuel, services, technology, plant design, and equipment for the commercial nuclear electric power industry. His mother worked for the *Penn-Franklin News*, a local newspaper, where she wrote a weekly humor column. Kilar has three brothers, James, Jeffrey, and Kenneth, and two sisters, Katie and Kerry.

Technology was always a part of Kilar's childhood. He told the *Pittsburgh Post-Gazette* in a 2012 interview that his family was among the first in their neighborhood to have an Apple IIe computer. "My dad was an early adopter of computers. You'd do connections over phone lines and take the phone off the hook and put it in these little black cups.... We were all set up with technology at home in ways

Kilar is shown here with his mother, Maureen, as they attend an awards ceremony.

most of my friends scratched their heads at. That had a heavy influence on me and gave me a real appreciation for how technology can be used to change things and improve people's lives," he said.

OBSESSED WITH WALT DISNEY

At nine years old, Kilar and his family drove from Pittsburgh to Orlando, Florida, to visit the Walt Disney World theme park for summer vacation. The trip inspired Kilar. "I had never seen something so high-quality," he said during a February 2013 appearance at his alma mater, the University of North Carolina at Chapel Hill. Kilar later told the *Pittsburgh Post-Gazette* that he grew up going to Kennywood, an amusement park in West Mifflin, Pennsylvania. "I thought that's what an amusement park was," he said of Kennywood. But when he walked onto Main Street at Disney World's Magic Kingdom Park, he was awestruck. In a keynote address at the NewTeeVee Live Conference in 2008, Kilar told the audience that Disney's obsession with quality was what he found so fascinating about Disney World. He was impressed with its spotlessness, with not one gum wrapper anywhere on the ground, to the park's attention to detail, from the look of the rides and storefronts, as all part of the overall Disney experience. "From that moment on I had to find out more: How was it created? How did it come to be?"

Kilar's first visit to Walt Disney World influenced how he developed Hulu into a user-friendly, interactive website with exceptional customer service.

Kilar quickly became obsessed with Walt Disney, the American animator who created Mickey Mouse and spawned a new era in entertainment with his theme parks. Kilar told the *Pittsburgh Post-Gazette*, "It's fair to say the notion of the world of Hollywood and storytelling is distant from what you're exposed to in Pittsburgh, but I was always fascinated as a kid by Walt Disney the entrepreneur."

In a November 2012 interview with *FastCompany*, Kilar talked about his interest in Disney: "I tried to do everything I could to study Walt Disney. I would read every book I could on the company, and then I'd found out more about him as a person, as an entrepreneur, and it was just fascinating to me that this guy was able to live a great life with his family but also do these amazing things at work." Kilar immersed himself in books about Disney's groundbreaking innovation with audio-animatronics, a form of robotic animation where robots moved and made noise, and the multi-plane camera, which is a film

Walt Disney pioneered exceptional customer service by implementing training for employees to be "assertively friendly," or seeking out ways to assist a guest before being asked. The Disney Institute offers courses for organizations to learn and implement the Disney service philosophy.

Who Was Walt Disney?

Walt Disney was an animator and cartoonist who later became a screenwriter, producer, director, and business entrepreneur. In 1923, Walt and his brother Roy founded the Disney Brothers Studio, which later became the Walt Disney Company. In 1928, Walt introduced an animated mouse, named Mickey, who became the star of several films, including *Steamboat Willie*, the company's first movie with sound. It was an instant hit and led to additional movies starring his animated mouse. In 1934, the company began production on the studio's first feature-length animated film. *Snow White and the Seven Dwarfs* was, at the time, the highest-grossing sound film. Disney moved his studio from Hollywood to Burbank, California, where it's still headquartered today. A string of successful animated films followed, including *Pinocchio* (1940), *Fantasia* (1940), *Dumbo* (1941), and *Bambi* (1942). In 1955, Walt opened Disneyland, in Anaheim, California, a place he imagined for both children and adults to enjoy together. In 1966, before Disney World in Orlando, Florida, was opened, Walt died. His brother Roy took over the company and in 1971, Disney World opened to the public. The theme parks feature rides, characters from Disney

(continued on the next page)

(continued from the previous page)

movies, and audio-animatronic figures. These robotic characters could move and speak, and they thrilled visitors. It was one of several ways that Walt Disney introduced innovation to the American public.

The Walt Disney Company today is a leader in film, animation, television production, theater, publishing, music, and online media. The company has expanded its theme parks around the world. Disney World theme parks are located in Tokyo, Paris, Hong Kong, and Shanghai. The company also runs the Disney Cruise Line, which features family-friendly cruises throughout the Caribbean, Alaska, the Mexican Riviera, and Europe.

process that creates a three-dimensional effect for animated productions. Kilar was fascinated by how Disney combined these technological advances with his storytelling to create depth and personality with animated movies and cartoons.

After learning as much as he could about Disney, Kilar realized that Disney's success could be attributed to the animator and businessman's relentless pursuit of finding better ways to do things, such as customer service, which is a hallmark of the Disney brand. Eventually,

Disney's dedication to improving everything he could became Kilar's personal definition of innovation.

EDUCATION

Kilar attended Franklin Regional High School, in Murrysville, Pennsylvania, until the middle of his junior year. His father took a job in Boca Raton, Florida, and the family moved south. Kilar saw the move as an opportunity. "Everybody says that must have been the worst possible thing, but it actually has been a blessing in that it taught me a lot about change and diversity and blooming where you're planted even if the pot changes from time to time," he told the *Pittsburgh Post-Gazette*. This kind of flexibility likely worked in Kilar's favor as he moved up the corporate ranks later in life.

After graduating from high school, Kilar attended the University of North Carolina at Chapel Hill for his undergraduate studies. There, he double majored in business administration, and journalism and mass communication. He credited UNC for giving him more than just an education in the subject areas he studied. Kilar said in a publication for UNC's Kenan-Flagler Business School that the school "did a very good job educating me about evaluating the current situation in business. 'Is it real? Is it meaningful? Can we have a sustained competitive advantage?'" He told the *Carolina Alumni Review* that among the experiences that shaped him during his time at

One of Jason Kilar's first jobs after he graduated from college was as a production assistant on the set of *The River Wild*, a film starring Meryl Streep, Kevin Bacon, and John C. Reilly.

UNC were his professors and the students he got to know there. He also credited the culture at Carolina, which he said showed him that "taking the high road, the hard-working path, was the way to go."

When he graduated from UNC, in 1993, Kilar's career aspirations were to get a job in Hollywood working on film sets. It was a direct result of the Walt Disney factor that influenced his life. He found job postings and sent out résumés and cover letters. When he received no responses, he decided to get creative. In an August 2009 article for the *New York Times*, Kilar described how he began sending out a comic strip of himself in place of a résumé. "I decided to draw a comic strip that showed me arriving in an envelope in the recipient's inbox, exiting the envelope, and using the office supplies on the manager's desk to show

how I could make a contribution," he wrote. The approach worked and he began getting calls and interviews. His first job after college was as a production assistant on the film *The River Wild*, a crime thriller starring Meryl Streep and Kevin Bacon. A few years later, Kilar returned to school to continue his education. He attended Harvard Business School, in Boston, Massachusetts, where he earned a Master of Business Administration (MBA) degree in 1997. In this program, Kilar learned advanced business management and leadership skills from courses that focused on developing a vision for your business, creating an organization to support your ideas, and using technology to further your business goals. These were all skills Kilar would put to use throughout his career.

FAMILY LIFE

The same month he graduated from UNC, Kilar's father passed away, at age forty-eight. His mother has remained in Florida, and his siblings are scattered across the United States.

During Kilar's senior year in college he met his future wife, Jamie. They dated for several years while Jason first worked at the Walt Disney Company, and then as he attended Harvard Business School. During this time, Jamie was earning a master's degree in pharmacy at UNC. They later married and had four children. Those who have worked with and for Kilar at Hulu consistently describe him as a family guy who will make sure he's home at night to tuck his children in.

EARLY CAREER

Before Kilar earned an MBA at Harvard Business School he spent three years working at the company of his idol, Walt Disney. He worked as an analyst in strategy and marketing for the Disney Design & Development Department. A marketing and strategy analyst is a business professional who studies and evaluates market trends. These analysts gather information about consumers and what they are interested in buying and why. They also research where a product might sell best. Their goals are to help a company determine what products it should introduce and how best to sell them. At the time the department was responsible for the design and construction of certain resort and shopping areas within Disney World. The department also planned the construction of a community in nearby Celebration, Florida. The Design & Development Department later became part of Disney's Imagineering Department. Kilar worked for Disney for two years, until 1995, when he left the company to pursue his graduate degree at Harvard Business School.

In one of his courses at Harvard, Kilar wrote a case study about Amazon. So when Jeff Bezos, Amazon's

As an executive at Amazon, Jason Kilar was in charge of creating user-friendly websites that excel at selling via the Amazon.com site. Shown here with Mark Stabingas (right), Kilar shows off the NBA store and Nordstrom sites that he helped to develop.

founder, came to campus to speak at an event, one of Kilar's professors arranged for Kilar to meet Bezos. The meeting must have been a successful one because Kilar later flew out to Seattle, Washington, Amazon's headquarters for an interview.

Kilar joined Amazon in 1997 as a product manager. In 1998, he wrote the business plan that led to the launch of Amazon Video & DVD, Amazon's online DVD and video rental/download service. Amazon Video & DVD was the precursor to Prime Instant Video, Amazon's own streaming video service. He rose quickly at Amazon, serving as vice president of Books, Music, and Video & DVD from February 2001 to October 2001, when he became vice president of the Marketplace. The Marketplace enables sellers to offer new and used items alongside Amazon's own inventory of products. In the Marketplace, customers shopping on Amazon can buy items directly from third-party sellers or from Amazon itself. During this time, Kilar did double duty. He was still vice president of the Books, Music, and Video & DVD division. In 2003, Kilar was named senior vice president of Amazon's Worldwide Application Software. He remained in that position until he left the company in 2006. This division dealt with media storage, cloud computing services, and Amazon's automated merchandising system.

Kilar decided to leave Amazon after nine years. He was ambitious and interested in developing his own company though he didn't launch right into a new venture. He traveled the world for a year, visiting nineteen countries and fifty-six cities with his wife and children. When he returned, he settled down to work in some rented office space. He had the beginnings of an idea about creating a media and technology company and needed time to work it out. But a few months into working out his own idea, he got a call from an executive search firm. Executive search firms work for companies to identify candidates for executive level positions. Kilar's work experience as a VP at Amazon, where he built a wealth of knowledge about the online consumer space, plus his work at the Disney Corporation, made him a highly desirable candidate. The recruiter explained that the company interested in speaking to him didn't even have an official name yet, which might have been discouraging. However, it was a joint venture between News Corp., NBC Universal, and Providence Equity Partners, a private investment company. Despite not having an official name, it was clear that it was no small starter company. After long conversations with Peter Chernin, then president and chief operating officer of News Corp., and Jeff Zucker who was the president and chief executive officer of NBC Universal, about their vision and goal for an online streaming video service, Kilar joined the team as the company's founding chief executive officer. Shortly afterward, in early 2008, Hulu was launched to the public.

CHAPTER 2

The Birth of Digital Television and the Internet

To understand how the success of Hulu came about, it's important to know a little about the history of digital television and the Internet, and the innovations that paved the way for a service like Hulu to exist.

Hulu capitalized on an evolving television landscape that has been changing for nearly forty years. Before 1975, if you wanted to watch a television show, you had to be in your living room, in front of your TV, at the time the show was airing. But over the years, a number of technologies changed both viewer behavior and viewer's expectations for when and how to watch favorite television shows. It all started with the introduction of the VCR.

TELEVISION WHEN YOU WANT IT

In 1975, the first mass-market VCR was introduced. The VCR, short for video cassette recorder, connected to the

The VHS tape introduced the idea of customer control. People could record a television show or sporting event and watch it later at a time convenient for them.

television and cable box. It allowed viewers to record a show on tape and watch it later. For the first time, television viewers had control over when they could watch shows. The VCR kept growing in popularity. By 1985, 57 percent of American homes had at least one VCR. Ten years later, that number had risen to 85 percent. In response to the growing popularity of watching shows on video, the movie industry made films available on tape for rental. Anyone could get the latest Hollywood films from neighborhood video stores for less than the price of a movie ticket. Video stores began to pop up all over the

United States as more and more people enjoyed movies from the comfort of home.

The late 1990s also saw the introduction of the Internet. The Internet was conceived in the late 1960s. It was used primarily by mathematicians in higher education and members of the technical community. Decades later, its widespread potential was recognized and the World Wide Web was introduced to the public in the late 1990s. During the same period, digitally based products, from video recorders (or digital camcorders) to digital cameras, were growing in popularity among consumers. As consumers began to document life events using digital media, they needed new ways of collecting and storing these new digital collections of home videos and photos. They also sought to find new ways to share digital images and video. Streaming video on a computer became the next step in the evolution toward Internet television. Video streaming software, like QuickTime and RealPlayer, has been available since the early 1990s. These software packages enabled people to film video on their digital camcorders of family events like birthday parties or vacations. They could edit the video using computer-based video editing software, and then upload it to their computer's hard drive to be enjoyed later.

Internet broadband grew. Broadband is the capacity for carrying data. It became possible to send images and other kinds of large data online, or house it on web pages.

Scientist Tim Berners-Lee is credited with inventing the World Wide Web in 1989. Since its inception, the Internet has changed the way people shop, conduct research, communicate, and be entertained.

Soon it was possible to stream video, and the Internet world was treated to its first network broadcast when *ABC World News* was streamed online in 1994. As the technology changed and companies realized the potential of the medium, a number of experiments with event-based webcasts followed. "Webcast" became the new catch-all word used to describe broadcasting content over the Internet. In 1995, the Macintosh New York Music Festival, sponsored by Apple, webcasted a series of concerts held in fifteen different clubs in New York. Later that year, Apple webcasted a Metallica concert from San Francisco on the Apple website. Around the world, other media companies began to experiment with webcasting on the Internet. In 1997, a David Bowie concert in London, England, was broadcast throughout Europe.

While it was a great leap forward for Internet content, these were all one-time-only events. Two upcoming innovations were going to be game changers for streaming video online: TiVo and YouTube. One would revolutionize when people watched television and the other changed what people could watch. But both would make it possible to stream regular content, versus one-time-only events.

THE END OF THE VCR

In 1999, TiVo was introduced to television viewers. Like a VCR, TiVo was a device that worked with a television and recorded programs for viewers to watch at a later time.

The difference, however, was that while a VCR recorded shows onto tape, TiVo recorded on a hard drive. It digitized and compressed analog video from any source, including broadcasts over antenna, delivered via cable box, or through direct broadcast satellite. TiVo's hard drive was similar to that of a computer, eliminating the need for people to continually buy tapes. While there were other types of digital video recorders (DVRs) on the market, TiVo offered more features than a traditional DVR. With TiVo, viewers controlled live TV with features like pause, fast forward, rewind, and instant replay. A traditional DVR could only record a show and play it back. TiVo continually taped the last thirty minutes of television automatically. This allowed viewers to pause and rewind up to a half hour of live television. It also allowed viewers to begin watching a show after it aired. Viewers could then fast-forward through commercials. TiVo viewers had access to even more content. A popular TiVo feature allowed two different programs to be recorded at the same time. These key features blew the humble VCR out of the water.

But while TiVo's features created a better user experience, its downfall was its interface. Customers complained about its complicated menu system and other obstacles that made it hard to view programming. Aside from these few difficulties, TiVo's innovation set the tone. Viewers clearly wanted to watch shows on their own time. They did not want to be at the mercy of a network's programming schedule. They also wanted to catch more shows with simultaneous recording on different channels. Opportunities for other innovations, including widespread digital TV, quickly followed.

CONTENT BY VIEWERS FOR VIEWERS

When Hulu was launched in 2008, streaming video was not a novelty for the Internet. It had actually been around in various forms, but began to gain traction in 1994, when technology was finally able to support this innovation. Up until the time Hulu emerged, streaming video hadn't been developed in a way that took advantage of current television and movie content. The closest to capitalize on that potential came in November 2005, when YouTube, a video-sharing website, was launched.

YouTube's content comes strictly from its users. They can record videos of almost anything and upload them to the site. From a child's first steps to cats playing the piano, user videos found success on the site, and the site found success with it. By July 2006, YouTube reported that users from around the world were uploading more than sixty-five thousand videos a day. More than one hundred million videos were being watched daily. Traditional television networks, like NBC, ABC, and CBS, took notice of YouTube's success, but they struggled to figure out how to use the new online medium to promote or repurpose their current television shows.

With the Internet came new ways to watch television, from on-demand services to streaming video, all of which allow viewers to control when and where they want to watch a television program or movie.

YouTube showed television networks and their executives that people were interested in creating content. More importantly, they would watch content via their computer screens.

It did not take long for the four major broadcast companies, NBC, ABC, CBS, and Fox, to realize that streaming video had the potential to impact their viewing audience. YouTube showed the networks a potential new business opportunity for streaming video online. But television studios wanted nothing to do with the website. Television networks viewed the site as a place for viewers to post content, not as a place to stream high-quality television productions. They also saw the site as a place rife with piracy of copyrighted material. Piracy is the unauthorized reproduction or use of anything copyrighted, from television shows and movies, to books, music, artwork, and logos. A copyright indicates when a piece of writing, video, etc. is owned by a certain person. It makes it illegal to steal someone else's work or ideas. Immediately networks began to see low-quality copies of shows or clips of shows on YouTube's site. They issued cease-and-desist orders to YouTube to remove the copyrighted material. Studios and television networks realized that while they may have to eventually put content online they scoffed at the idea that their high-quality television shows and movies would be viewed in the same space as low-quality home videos of random content—all those cat videos! In addition, they knew advertisers would not be interested in creating ads for this online space, where they could not track the demographics of who they were reaching.

The launch of Hulu and its leadership by Jason Kilar was the answer to many of these concerns.

MOVIES BY DELIVERY

In 1997, another player emerged on the scene and had an impact on on-demand services. Netflix started out as a mail-order movie rental service. Customers paid a flat fee and

YouTube by the Numbers

YouTube has an impressive list of statistics:

- 800 million people visit the site per month.

- 4 billion videos are viewed each day.

- 60 hours of video are uploaded to YouTube every minute.

- 30 percent of YouTube traffic comes from the United States; 70 percent from around the world.

- 39 countries get YouTube in 54 different languages.

- 1 trillion views in 2011 translated to roughly 140 views for every person on the planet that year.

- 999 million (and counting) views makes Justin Bieber's song "Baby" (featuring Ludacris) the most popular YouTube video.

created an online list of movies they wanted to view at home. Netflix delivered the top movie on a customer's list to his or her home via the postal service. Customers could keep the movie as long as they wanted without risk of late fees. After customers mailed the movie back in a prepaid envelope, the next film on their list was automatically sent out. When Netflix launched, it had an initial archive of 925 movies. In 2004, with nearly two-thirds of American homes having at least one DVD player, Netflix saw interest in its company expand. By 2005, the company offered more than thirty-five thousand film titles and had introduced a monthly subscription. Customers could now pay a monthly fee for an unlimited number of rentals. In 2007, the company began offering video on demand via the Internet. Customers could now log onto the Netflix website and choose a movie to watch instantly online or on a mobile device.

Prime Instant Video, Amazon's own streaming video service, also began to grow in popularity. The service originally offered on-demand video to consumers. They could download videos to their desktop or watch them via the Amazon website. Each download had an expiration date that was usually within twenty-four hours of renting a video.

The successes and challenges of TiVo, YouTube, Netflix, and even Prime Instant Video created an opportunity for the right company to come along and merge the viewer experience of TiVo (watching content when you wanted to) with the on-demand services of Netflix and Amazon, and the streaming video presence of YouTube. That company was Hulu.

THE LAUNCH OF HULU

Hulu's online video-streaming service is, in some respects, the best of TiVo, YouTube, and Netflix. At its

Netflix began as a direct-mail service, where customers were delivered movies via the postal service but evolved into an almost entirely online streaming service.

launch, Hulu allowed people to watch TV and movies via their computers. The company later added tablets and mobile phones to the list of user devices. At first the site offered shows that previously aired on network television. If viewers missed, say, the previous night's episode of *The Simpsons* or that week's episode of *Glee*, they could get it from Hulu. This approach proved popular with viewers and in its second year of operation, Hulu was ranked No. 7 among all streaming sites in the United States.

Its popularity also made Hulu a strong competitor of YouTube. However, both sites have major differences. YouTube is primarily a video-sharing website. Anyone can open an account and post a video they shot themselves. By contrast, Hulu streams television productions, including sitcoms, dramas, and other television shows, that are professionally produced and edited by studios.

When Hulu launched, technology experts argued that it was doomed to fail. They doubted that people would want to watch TV shows on small computer screens. They felt the success of YouTube meant people turned to the Internet for user-generated content, not previously aired TV. They also felt that Hulu's backers of different media companies would compete. They imagined that each company would have its own agenda. Experts expected the companies to clash. They

Online Viewing Habits

Just how popular are online video-streaming services such as Hulu and Netflix? A 2013 study by Nielsen, a company that looks at television viewing numbers, revealed how prevalent online viewership is among the top streaming websites.

- 38 percent of Americans use or subscribe to Netflix.

- 18 percent of Americans use Hulu, with 12 percent saying they use the free version and 6 percent using the subscription-based Hulu Plus.

- 13 percent of Americans said they use Amazon Prime Instant Video.

- 88 percent of Netflix users reported watching three or more episodes of a TV show in a single day; 45 percent said they watch Netflix's original series on streaming services, *House of Cards* or *Orange Is the New Black*.

- Among all Netflix users, 48 percent watch on a computer screen; 23 percent watch on a smartphone; and 15 percent watch on their iPad.

wondered if disagreements would result from which network's shows got more airplay. But the experts didn't count on Kilar's ability to lead.

Heading Hulu wasn't simple, but Jason Kilar made it all work. He marketed Hulu as the place to go for network TV. He didn't compete with YouTube, which was where viewers went for content that wasn't on their television sets. Kilar also worked with NBC and Fox, and later Disney when they joined in 2009, to hammer out differences in what the three networks wanted. He eventually led Hulu as a unit with a singular vision.

Kilar also lead the design of an easy-to-use website with an innovative video player function, and he created a new way for advertisers to reach their audience.

What helped Hulu succeed was its approach to using content. At first the challenge Hulu faced with studios and networks was whether new content should be created for this medium, or if current content should be reused. It was a similar scenario movie studios faced in the 1940s and '50s, when television began to quickly grow in popularity. Movie studios needed to decide how to distribute their films and how best to work television into the mix. Now a standard agreement dictates movie distribution. A movie is first in theaters. Then it goes to pay television networks, such as HBO, Showtime, or Cinemax. Television broadcast is the final step. But for streaming video services like Hulu, these details were not worked out. This was one thing Kilar could not streamline. There is still some inconsistency in how each network allows its content to be used. Jason Kilar soon learned that each studio and network was doing its own thing and making the rules up as it went. Some made shows available the day after they aired. Some demanded an eight-day delay. Still others decided only to air their content on their own websites. This bypassed Hulu and other online streaming sites altogether.

CHAPTER 9

Hulu Revolutionizes Television Viewing

Jason Kilar's vision for Hulu transformed streaming video on the Internet. Under his leadership, Hulu grew from a single website offering previously aired TV to a service featuring content from more than four hundred partners. It had network and cable TV series, the latest film releases, and original programming from top television producers and filmmakers. One of Kilar's goals was to make Hulu user-friendly. He achieved this by paying attention to details that customers liked. These included Hulu's video player, which was larger than usual. It also meant television and movie content offered in high definition, or HD. Networks were upset when he rejected older shows from the studio's libraries. They did not meet Kilar's quality standards. Eventually, the networks caved. His decision to only air content in HD forced networks to improve the way they encoded their content, which meant Hulu's viewers were getting the best viewing experience possible. Hulu's viewers also watched fewer ads than they would on TV and had control over which they preferred to see. As a result, Hulu grew dramatically in popularity. It also helped change the television industry as a whole.

THE END OF TRADITIONAL TELEVISION?

There has been an ongoing conflict between the owners of digital media and the people who want access to it. As streaming video on the Internet grew in popularity, so did piracy. Piracy is the illegal use of copyrighted material. It could be airing copyrighted content on other sites, like some of YouTube's viewers did. It could mean repurposing images for unauthorized uses. Some television watchers were recording episodes of shows and movies from their televisions and uploading them to YouTube or other websites for wider distribution. Many media companies recognized this as a threat and sought to protect and control their content. NBC Universal and News Corp., which owns the Fox Television network, saw the creation of Hulu as an answer to this issue. What they didn't expect was the impact Hulu and other online streaming video service providers would have on traditional television.

TV generates more than $70 billion in advertising revenue annually. Cable companies still pay content providers tens of billions of dollars in licensing and subscription fees. So while Hulu's revenue would not threaten network

CBS's *The Big Bang Theory* is TV's most watched comedy, with more than eighteen million people watching current episodes live on Thursday nights (when the show originally airs) or via on demand in the days following a new show.

and cable television, the loss of viewers could. At its peak, Hulu had roughly forty-three million unique visitors a month. These viewers were eating away at television's audience. Television ratings remain at an all-time low, according to a November 2013 article in *Business Insider.* The four major broadcast networks are facing increased competition from multiple competitors offering alternative viewing choices. Cable networks, such as AMC and HBO, are producing top-notch shows and drawing viewers like never before. The season premiere of AMC's drama *The Walking Dead* drew more than twenty million viewers. In 2013, it was the most-watched scripted television show on cable. Those kinds of numbers are often reserved for top comedies and dramas on the four main networks, like CBS's *The Big Bang Theory,* which was television's most watched comedy in 2013. It averaged eighteen million viewers an episode. This growth in cable ratings represented a shift in both viewer interest and quality content available in places other than the networks. In the past, cable networks were known for a narrower focus. They might run syndicated television shows, such as reruns of once-popular sitcoms. Some were content specific, such as airing news, weather, or business-related information. Original programming was a threat to network television.

The other threat was free and subscription-based content. Hulu, Netflix, and Amazon were offering this to customers. Hulu Plus charges $7.99 a month, without a contract, for access to the full current seasons of shows on some very popular network and cable channels. It also provides access to an extensive library of back seasons of top shows. Added to that is a library of movies. All content on Hulu Plus is presented in HD. That means it can be streamed in high quality using a wide range of devices, including computers, mobile devices such as a smartphone or tablet, and game consoles such as Wii, Xbox, and

What Does "Hulu" Mean Anyway?

According to the Hulu website, in a blog post written by Jason Kilar, Kilar explains why they chose the name Hulu: "In Mandarin, *Hulu* has two interesting meanings, each highly relevant to our mission. The primary meaning interested us because it is used in an ancient Chinese proverb that describes the Hulu as the holder of precious things. It literally translates to 'gourd,' and in ancient times, the Hulu was hollowed out and used to hold precious things. The secondary meaning is 'interactive recording.' We saw both definitions as appropriate bookends and highly relevant to the mission of Hulu."

PlayStation 3. It was also available on streaming media devices such as Roku and Internet-enabled Blue-ray players and televisions in addition to a variety of other media devices.

Similarly, Netflix, which has always been subscription-based, has a significant library of movies but has fewer choices when it comes to television shows. However, its library of television content is growing just as Hulu's film library is expanding. The service is also $7.99 per month with no contract. Netflix can also stream to a wide range of media devices, gaming consoles, and mobile devices. The downside to both of these services is that some content, particularly sports, cannot be viewed at all using these providers. Avid sports fans still have to go to the major television networks or traditional cable companies.

Netflix has also grown in popularity due to the success of two of its original scripted series. *Orange Is the New Black*, a comedy about women in prison, and *House of Cards*, a political drama, are both critically acclaimed series. Both have also drawn more viewers to Netflix, which is the only place these shows are aired.

Since Hulu's launch in 2008, network television viewership is down 12.5 percent. It is estimated that more than five million American homes have abandoned their cable subscriptions since 2010 in exchange for watching content over the Internet. The decline in viewers affects how much networks make from advertising.

Hulu has changed the world of advertising, using subscribers' demographics to send targeted ads and allowing viewers to select the commercials they want to see.

THE BUSINESS OF TELEVISION

Networks don't own TV shows; they license them from TV studios. TV studios produce shows. For example, CBS is a production company that produces television shows that are sold to a number of networks, such as CBS, the CW, or USA Network. Some of its shows, like *The Amazing Race, Hawaii Five-0, NCIS, The Vampire Diaries, The Originals*, and *Hart of Dixie,* are then licensed, or sold to networks, which air them on TV. A license lets a network air the show for a certain number of year; spells out how many times per year a network is allowed to run the show; and how or if the network is able to use the show in other media outlets, such as the Internet. A television network makes its money by selling commercial space, or advertising time, during each show to companies that want to promote their products or services. The more popular a show, the more money a network can charge for a commercial. A larger audience means a wider range of viewers is watching a show, so companies reach a bigger audience for their product.

Advertising revenue is also how Hulu makes money. Kilar pioneered a new business model for placing ads on streaming video, and it was his vision behind the success of Hulu's advertising business model. He began placing ads on both Hulu's free and subscription-based services. Instead of the eight minutes of commercials networks place in a twenty-two-minute sitcom, Hulu offered only four minutes of commercials. And he made it possible for viewers to select which ads they wanted to see. According to Hulu's own statistics, 96 percent of the ads presented to viewers are being watched in full.

Hulu does not pay its content providers (such as NBC or Fox) licensing fees for its shows. Instead, it gives them a share of the advertising revenue it earns. This is a different business model from how traditional television networks make money.

Hulu changed the business of television and made streaming video a profitable entity. Hulu has more than one thousand advertisers. The site also boasts a very attractive demographic of viewers. Demographics are the age, income, ethnicity, and other identifying characteristics of viewers. According to Nielsen, Hulu's users are young, tech-savvy viewers with an average annual income of $75,000. For those who subscribe to Hulu Plus, the average annual income rises to $100,000. Hulu commands a premium price for commercial spots on its programs. Typically, Hulu charges its advertisers $30 to $35 per thousand views of a show, with up to $50 for more popular shows. Hulu's ads are 90 percent more effective than traditional online video spots, thanks to Kilar's innovative "Ad Swap." The idea behind this was that viewers knew their interest best, so they should choose the ads they want to view. He also made sure that Hulu was tracking viewing and video consumption habits. Hulu then used this data to determine the best ads to present to an individual viewer. In other words, car commercials were targeting young men, while beauty product ads were targeting young women.

KILAR GOES TO THE SOURCE

In addition to an innovative advertising system, Kilar focused on growing Hulu's content. He met regularly with network executives to pitch them the idea behind Hulu. He also reached out to showrunners directly. A showrunner is the person who is responsible for the day-to-day operation of a television series. He or she are the source of show content. Kilar contacted showrunners from some of the most popular shows on network television, including Joss

Whedon, who created and serves as executive producer of *Marvel's Agents of SH.I.E.L.D.*, and Seth MacFarlane, who created, wrote, and produced *Family Guy*. When Kilar reached out to Whedon and MacFarlane, network

Family Guy creator Seth MacFarlane worked directly with Hulu to provide content for the site.

executives saw this as Kilar stepping on their turf. But Kilar made them understand how Hulu was good for both the networks and content creators. While network executives were not happy with Kilar for going directly to show creators, people like Whedon and Mac-Farlane were. They saw an opportunity to create content that maintained their original vision. Oftentimes a show creator must get approval from a network for certain storylines. Scripts often undergo a review by the network. Creators may need to make revisions that the network wants, even if they disagree. In the end, Kilar ended up getting cool content created just for Hulu. Whedon and John Cassaday, an illustrator and art director, released their graphic novel, *Astonishing X-Men*, as a motion comic on Hulu. MacFarlane created and starred in an ad promoting Hulu.

Kilar attracted hundreds of content partners, growing Hulu's library to 870 different TV shows and close to 500 movies. "We would go visit everybody we could possibly meet, just to make sure people understood why we thought this was good for them as networks and as content creators," Kilar told *FastCompany* in November 2012. By the fall of 2009, Hulu had become the

Trends in Online Consumer Viewing

Every year, Accenture, a management consulting and technology company, produces a Video-Over-Internet Consumer Survey. The survey looks at the trends and habits of consumers using streaming video. The 2013 results show that online video viewing has grown into a popular, mainstream activity. Nearly 90 percent of consumers surveyed watched video over the Internet. The survey also reveals other key facts about consumers and their viewing habits:

- The computer (desktop and laptop) remains the most popular way to view online content.

- Tablets are growing in popularity. In the 2013 survey, one-third of consumers reported watching video on a tablet. That's an increase over 2012's 21 percent of viewers using tablets.

- Multitasking is growing. Forty-four percent of people say they watch television while also using a mobile device, such as a smartphone or tablet.

Streaming video got a boost with the introduction of the tablet computer, which enabled people to travel with their favorite shows and stream them on a larger screen.

- When it comes to watching streaming video content via their television sets, only 31 percent of people say they understand the technology and are willing to install the devices needed to do this.

second-most-popular video hub online and the only one with a clear business model. In 2009, *Entrepreneur* magazine put Kilar on its list of 25 Innovators in Technology for his vision and innovative use of technology in building Hulu into a leading video content provider.

But Kilar's vision for content didn't stop with recruiting showrunners and network shows. He saw original content as the next stepping-stone to gaining more viewers. In February 2012, Hulu debuted its first original scripted comedy, *Battleground*, a show about a Wisconsin political campaign. In March 2012, the service kicked off the second season of *A Day in the Life*. This docuseries, or documentary-style television series, is created and directed by filmmaker Morgan Spurlock. Spurlock was best known for the hit documentaries *Supersize Me*, *The Greatest Movie Never Sold*, and *30 Days*. His new show for Hulu takes viewers into the world of a celebrity in each episode. The second season included actor-comedian Joel McHale, the host of the TV show *Talk Soup*. The director rounded up a diverse group of celebrities. He had cooking-show host Mario Batali, music star Questlove, and UFC fighter Jason "Mayhem" Miller. Kilar also attracted filmmakers such as Richard Linklater, who produced a travel show for Hulu called *Up to Speed*. The variety show *Spoilers* came from director Kevin Smith. It mixed movie reviews, comedy, and audience involvement. Smith is well known for acting in and producing movies such as *Good Will Hunting*, *Clerks*, and *Dogma*.

As of 2014, Hulu offers nine original series: *A Day in the Life, Battleground, Spoilers, Up to Speed, The Awesomes, Quick Draw, The Wrong Mans, Behind the Mask*, and *The Hotwives of Orlando*.

THE CUSTOMER-FIRST APPROACH

Taking a lesson from Walt Disney, Kilar told the *Pittsburgh Post-Gazette*, "The most important thing we need to do is remain relentlessly focused on the customer." For Kilar, that meant carefully looking at three distinct groups: end users watching Hulu, advertisers spending money to air commercials on the site, and content providers and owners who showcase their programs on Hulu. In the same interview, Kilar added that working with content providers was the key to Hulu's long-term success: "Our content partners are our customers, and I personally spend a tremendous amount of time on that. Content creators are very courageous: They believe in a story, in a writer, in a director, and invest collectively $40 billion in creating television series and feature films annually.... The way we think about our job is to make sure we're making them make a fair return on their investment. Ultimately we are aligned."

CHAPTER 4

Where Are the Viewers Watching?

A study by Nielsen in February 2014 found that while television still dominates the devices used to view media, more and more people are choosing other devices. The survey reported that, on average, most American viewers own four digital devices. That could include any combination of a high-definition television set, Internet-connected computers or smartphones, digital video recorders (DVRs), and gaming consoles. Across these multiple devices, viewers spend an average of sixty hours a week watching television shows. This shift is causing an increase in the type of devices that can carry television shows and improve the user experience.

VIEWERS IN CONTROL

Hulu is certainly not the only place where consumers can watch streaming video content. In addition to Netflix, almost every major broadcast company has developed

The Apple iPhone changed the mobile phone landscape in dramatic ways, enabling people to access the Internet more easily and use their phone for business and entertainment.

their own Internet distribution arms. While this increases the competition among sites to provide the best user experience, the real winners are viewers. They now have more control of their viewing than ever before.

In an April 4, 2012, interview with the *Pittsburgh Post-Gazette*, Kilar commented on how Internet streaming video is affecting technology. He talked about how several new devices can assist consumers in streaming video content to their televisions. He also discussed how these devices can integrate with each other. "I think it's taking so long because one of the rarest skills in the tech-media industry is the ability to simplify," he said in the interview. "The most fascinating transition I've seen as an adult was the transition from smartphones to the iPhone. There were smartphones before the iPhone...but the iPhone made it simple and intuitive. People look at it now and say, 'I can't imagine my life without this thing. Why didn't people do this before?' There are rumors about Apple [developing a new TV device], but I also think there isn't a major television manufacturer who isn't hard at work on a smart television set...The question is: Who's the first to get there?"

Manufacturers are working on developing television sets that will interact directly with the Internet. In the meantime, a variety of devices have become available. Each helps to connect different kinds of technology to improve the user experience and increase consumers' choices for access to content.

NEW VIEWING TECH

Kilar sees the future of streaming video not only with online content services like Hulu, Netflix, and networks' own websites, but also over a wide range of devices. Several types of devices are delivering content to TV sets like never before. Consumers have a lot to choose from.

STREAMING VIDEO BOXES

A streaming box is similar to a cable box in that it connects your television set to the Internet. The devices, many of which cost $100 or less, are compatible with any TV set that has HDMI. Short for high-definition multimedia interface, HDMI transfers digital video and audio signals to a high-definition or digital television. Many new television sets are already high definition. Those that aren't can still receive digital broadcasts. An HDMI cable helps connect older television sets with the digital signals that television networks and digital devices now use.

While all streaming video boxes work with HDTVs, some may also work with older television sets. The purpose of a streaming video box is to stream online content from the web to a television set so that programs are available on a full TV screen. Streaming video boxes provide access to the extensive digital media libraries offered by service providers like Hulu or Netflix. The most popular ones on the market today are Apple TV, Roku, and Google Chromecast.

Streaming boxes allow customers to play through their televisions games that were once only available on their phones.

Apple TV gives consumers access to streaming video from not only online content providers but also from other Apple devices. So any content downloaded onto an iPhone, iPad, or iPod Touch can be accessed and watched on television via Apple TV. The content does not have to be bought again. The device connects to any high-definition TV set and works using WiFi. WiFi allows an electronic device to connect to and exchange data on the Internet without being physically connected via wire or cords. Apple TV comes ready for access to iTunes, Apple's library of movies and music, plus a range of online content providers, several Disney networks, and some sports, news and other entertainment sites. Apple TV also uses iCloud, Apple's digital storage service. iCloud connects to all Apple devices and enables each to access photos, music, apps, movies, documents, and more. Apple TV can stream a collection of photos stored on iCloud. It can just as easily stream a movie you downloaded to your iPhone. iCloud connects users to their entire library of content, all of the time.

Roku is a device with four different models. Each is based on the price and number of available content providers. Roku is a streaming video box that supports access to more than one thousand channels, including Netflix, Amazon Instant, HBO Go, Hulu Plus, Pandora, Amazon Cloud Player, Vudu, and YouTube. It also carries a wide selection of sports and entertainment sites. It can access apps and games, allowing you to use an app or play video games that were once only available on your phone. The Roku Channel store has an extensive list of online content providers, free channels, and premium channels. That includes Hulu Plus, Netflix, Disney Channel, numerous sports channels, and entertainment and news networks. It also allows access to a wide range of games. Customers can play *Angry Birds*, one of the most popular gaming apps of all time, or classic games like *Galaga* and *Pac-Man*. Once customers set up a Roku, they select the channels or networks they want access to. For premium channels, such as Hulu Plus, there is a subscription to gain access to the site's online content. A downside of the Roku is that it doesn't always work well with Apple products. Integration with an Apple smartphone or tablet, such as the iPhone or iPad, may produce access problems.

The Google Chromecast is a small device that plugs into the USB port of your computer or TV. It streams to your TV by using nearly any smartphone or tablet. The Chromecast is a basic streaming video device that doesn't allow a wide range of connections to various sites or apps. It doesn't come with a remote control, and there are also no on-screen interface. Access and control of the device are dependent on a smartphone or tablet. Its small size means you can take it with you when you travel. It also fits easily behind your television, versus taking up space next to or near your TV set. Currently the Chromecast is intended for those who want basic streaming video service but are not interested in all the extended amenities like games, apps, and multiple online content providers.

There are reports on tech websites that Amazon is developing its own streaming video box. It will connect customers to Amazon Instant Video. This is the website's own streaming video library that Amazon Prime members have access to now via their laptops and smartphones.

HYBRID SERVICES

In addition to streaming video boxes, another device to consider is the Aereo. Aereo is basically a very small TV antenna. For a monthly fee, it allows a customer to watch TV live or record television programs to a cloud, or online server, for viewing later. Aereo is limited to the area where a customer lives. It works off the antennas in the area. At sign-up, customers are assigned to two local antennas. One is for watching live shows and the other is for recording programs. Local over-the-air shows are streamed to a digital video recorder (DVR)–like service on a cloud service.

Aereo does not have a license to transmit or record copyrighted programs. That includes all the programming available on network television. Originally, the ABC network filed a lawsuit against Aereo over its content distribution. Eventually, other major networks joined the suit, including NBC. The Supreme Court decision of June 25, 2014 said that Aereo violated copyright law by using antennas to broadcast television to their paying customers. The decision may make it harder for other internet-based broadcasting to provide content.

GAMING CONSOLES

Gaming consoles, like Microsoft's Xbox, Sony's PlayStation 3, and Nintendo's Wii, are now more than just game

Gaming consoles like the Xbox, which can play games as well as connect to the Internet, now also stream video.

playing. More and more they are used to stream video content from online sources.

Every year, the E3 conference brings together gamers and the latest games and gaming tech. In 2012, companies that made consoles were targeting not just excited gamers, but television viewers as well. They were actively pitching new apps that can turn gaming consoles into a multimedia platform. In a study by the Leichtman Research Group, Microsoft reported that those who own an Xbox 360 spend more time online watching videos and listening to music than playing games. Just four years ago, playing video games was the only thing you could do with a game console. According to a June 5, 2012, article in the *Los Angeles Times*, more than forty million people use the Xbox Live online service. More than fifty-one million PlayStation 3 consoles are connected to Sony's free Internet service. Now people can also connect to Hulu, Netflix, HBO Go, and other online service providers to access streaming content that they can play on their television sets.

Ross Honey, general manager of Xbox Live entertainment and advertising, told the *Los Angeles Times* that "entertainment has always been part of our strategy, but it was in the background. Now we have the content and user experience to legitimately tell a consumer, 'This is the platform for all of your entertainment.'"

Understanding TV Ratings

Television networks, including cable networks, get regular reports on how many people are watching their shows. The Nielsen Company gathers and reports such data. Nielsen looks at a specific number of households in a number of cities around the country. It asks a wide range of families to participate in their data tracking. It looks for different kinds of families.

(continued on the next page)

The tablet is now a common sight in many places, as it enables users to connect easily to the Internet for a wide range of uses, from entertainment and travel directions, to streaming video and online lesson plans.

(continued from the previous page)

Getting information from people of different backgrounds, from all parts of the country, and of different ages, is important. It also looks for different family groupings, like single child, single parent, etc. This way, it can get a more accurate assessment of who is watching what. For example, a family with toddlers may be watching cartoons or educational programming. A household with teenage boys might have more interest in sporting events. Nielsen collects their viewing information in a variety of ways:

- *Viewer participation*: Nielsen regularly asks families and individuals to participate in its tracking system. For a specific period of time, Nielsen tracks what they are watching on each television set.

- *Cross-platform reporting*: Nielsen's cross-platform reporting takes into account viewership of programs through DVR recording and Internet viewing. However, the company says that its ratings information for cross-platform viewing is incomplete.

An added benefit of using a gaming console to stream video content is that it cuts down on the number of devices people need for entertainment.

TRACKING VIEWERS

Finding out where the viewers have gone is critical to networks. Ratings have always been the indication of success for television shows. Shows are cancelled for poor viewership. Others are given additional seasons if viewers are tuning in. This is also how networks make money. Networks sell advertising during these popular shows. Consider the problem that DVRs and online streaming has created for networks. Where do they get their viewership numbers? In the current television season alone, Nielsen has tracked a trend in people watching shows several days after they initially air. This is called time-shifted viewing. ABC's *Marvel's Agents of S.H.I.E.L.D.*, NBC's *The Blacklist*, and Fox's *Sleepy Hollow* have all posted record-setting viewership for people watching the shows three to seven days later via their DVR. Nielsen is able to track two distinct ratings for time-shifted shows. Live +3 tracks the numbers for views up to three days. This includes viewers who watch the show live, plus any viewership that happens in the next three-day period. Live +7 accounts for the live airing, plus viewership during the following seven-day period.

Nielsen's reach is still limited. It cannot track viewers who use streaming video services like Hulu, Netflix, or Amazon. So there is no way to confirm the number of viewers that are watching the show via streaming video. These new media outlets are presenting a challenge to the traditional ways in which ratings are tracked for shows.

Netflix in particular is highly secretive about how many people are watching its shows. Two of its original shows, *House of Cards* and *Orange Is the New Black*, are earning critical reviews. But no one really knows how many people are tuning in to watch these programs. In a September 2013 article in *Forbes* magazine, Netflix executives say they don't release ratings information because they don't have to. Since the service does not sell advertising space, like Hulu, and relies instead on subscription fees for revenue, it doesn't need to share its ratings to secure advertisers. So it chooses not to. Without ratings information, there is no way to know if Netflix's original programming is really as popular as it appears to be.

CHAPTER 5

Different Viewing Means Different Advertising

The cost of advertising has to do with how many people are watching a show, but advertisers need to be sure they are targeting the right consumers. The Nielsen Company not only provides ratings, but also data about what people are watching and where. It also tracks who the viewers are and can identify the demographics, or the makeup of the viewers of a show. The demographics for sports shows, for example, mostly consist of men. For years, television's captive audience made Nielsen's job somewhat easy. But when a portion of viewers has shifted away from traditional television in favor of streaming video and on demand services, how can a company target them effectively? Jason Kilar found a way.

Kilar was known to have checked Twitter constantly to see what customers were saying. He used the feedback to make changes to services or deliver content that people wanted.

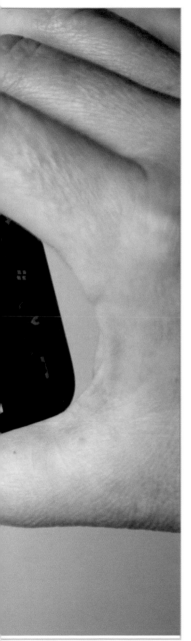

CUSTOMER-CONTROLLED ADVERTISING

Jason Kilar's focus was always on his customers, in particular the viewing experience of his audience. In his time at Hulu, he was known for checking Twitter consistently throughout the day to see what people were saying about the company. In a November 2009 article in *FastCompany*, Kilar explained, "I've always said that our brand is what people say about us when we're not in the room, and [Twitter] is the best tool for hearing what people are saying." Twitter is a social networking and blogging site where participants tweet, or say something, in 140 characters or less. People can follow one another to see what they are saying. Hashtags, or # signs, allow people to follow all tweets about a subject, such as #hulu. Anyone can have a Twitter account, including individuals, television shows, companies, and corporations. As of February 2014, Hulu's Twitter account has more than 109,000 followers. As Kilar monitored feedback from the Hulu audience via Twitter, the information helped him and his team deliver programming relevant to their audience. This approach also helped him target this audience for advertising.

While broadcast TV remains the most effective way to reach an audience for advertisers, the online audience is growing. This makes online viewers another segment of the population that advertisers are eager to reach. According to the *FastCompany* article, advertising by broadcast networks, which includes the four major networks plus cable networks, rakes in around $46 billion annually. That is for ad space on television. Advertising spending online, which is growing by 43 percent each year, still only accounts for $1 billion annually. What advertisers need is to figure out which platforms attract the biggest audience.

One way Hulu has attracted viewers is by showing fewer ads per show than the networks. Hulu shows just two minutes of advertising for a thirty-minute sitcom,

Since people, including teenagers, live on their phones, this is the easiest way to monitor changing trends, including the shift from television viewing to online viewing of shows and movies.

versus eight minutes shown on a network. Hulu also limits advertising to one sponsor per show. This increases what viewers recall of the ad. Recall, or remembering what you saw or heard, is a key metric for advertisers. It tells product companies that their audience remembered specifics of their ad, such as the product's name or its distinguishable features, which means they have effectively reached their audience and raised awareness of their product. For networks, where one ad might be buried amid several during every commercial break, getting specific attention from an audience that is only watching one company's ads can give valuable data. Jean-Paul Colaco, Hulu's senior vice president of advertising, told *FastCompany* that limiting sponsorship to one advertiser per episode helps make recall rates twice as high as those for the same ads on TV. The article also cites ad buyers who say that level of customer engagement with an ad has helped Hulu increase ad rates to 50 to 100 percent higher per thousand viewers than broadcast rates.

Part of this stronger reach comes from Kilar's idea to let the Hulu audience be an active participant of the advertising experience. In many cases, Hulu watchers can choose which commercials to watch, instead of being fed a lineup of commercials based on marketing research. Viewers also get to decide how they want to watch ads. They can watch ads in one long segment before a movie or television program begins, or they can watch ads in shorter segments, during breaks in a program. Viewers can also vote on ads, which helps Hulu provide viewer feedback to the advertisers. This is another added value for companies that want to know what consumers are thinking. In addition to viewer feedback, Hulu uses demographic information to select ads for its viewers. When you register an account with Hulu, it gathers information about who you are, such as your date of birth and gender. Hulu also tracks what its audience is watching, which can further help advertisers target their audience. If they find a large segment of men between the ages of eighteen and thirty-five are watching *The Blacklist*, this can tell Hulu which ads will best reach the audience watching this particular show. Hulu's entire concept of advertising enables product companies to reach a more precise audience that broadcast television can provide. "I have a big belief that if you don't have children under the age of 2, you don't need to see a Pampers commercial," Kilar told *FastCompany* about Hulu's advertising strategy. "That's not money well spent for an advertiser."

In the same article, Kilar acknowledges that for Hulu to stay competitive and earn revenue that will enable it to continue to provide the content viewers want, it will likely have to increase the amount of advertising on its shows.

Hulu's Programming

In addition to Hulu's growing original scripted content, the following list is a sample of the networks and companies Hulu receives programming from:

Networks

- Fox Broadcasting Network: The Fox Network, FX, Fox News Channel, Fox Business Network, and the National Geographic Channel.

- NBC Universal: The NBC Network, CNBC, MSNBC, SyFy, and Oxygen.

- Walt Disney Company: The ABC Network and ABC Family.

- A&E Television Networks: The A&E, The Biography Channel, and the History Channel.

- Turner Broadcasting System/Warner Brothers: The TBS, TNT, the Cartoon Network, truTV, CNN, Adult Swim, and The CW.

- AMC Networks: The AMC Channel

- ION Television

- Food Network: The Cooking Channel

Producers and Distributors

- NBCUniversal
- DreamWorks SKG
- Endemol
- Cablevision
- ABC
- 21st Century Fox
- Sony Pictures
- Time Warner
- Nutri Ventures Corporation

Exclusive Hulu Content

Hulu also has exclusive rights to these shows that cannot be found anywhere else online:

- *All My Children*
- *One Life to Live*
- *The Fashion Fund*
- *Prisoners of War*
- *Spy*
- *The Yard*

NETWORKS TRYING TO CONTROL HULU VIA CONTENT

Hulu is in an awkward position of being at the intersection of old television and new television. Networks and cable companies worry that if their audience can watch the same show on Hulu with fewer ads, they could become intolerant of ads on TV. The term "convergence" is a television industries term. It means making high-quality online video available on TV. In a 2009 *FastComapny* interview, Jeff Zucker, who was president of NBC Universal at the time, said that Hulu was pulling viewers: "In some form, that's clearly going to happen. It's a question of how we navigate that migration."

As viewers asserted more control over their viewing experience, the networks began stepping in to try to control what content they were allowing Hulu to have access to in an attempt to slow the traffic of viewers moving away from TV. Networks began to limit how much content they were willing to provide to Hulu.

For Kilar's team, getting content for Hulu was not as simple as asking the networks for it. Networks, cable companies, and production studios want to maximize revenue in every way possible for each show, even each episode, through advertising, licensing fees, DVD sales, and syndication. They don't want to make content available if it will lessen their ability to make money. As a

Jeff Zucker, president and CEO of NBC, understood that online viewership was pulling viewers away from traditional television and wanted to find a way to make that work for the networks.

result, Hulu has had to work with what it's been given when it comes to content. Each network has been doing things a little differently, but in general, content comes to Hulu in one of several ways. For current shows, Hulu has exclusive rights to only the last five episodes. For shows with previously aired seasons, Hulu might have some full seasons and some partial seasons. For new shows that are searching for an audience, a network might use Hulu to generate interest.

Even within a content provider, there are no rules. Fox, which owns the TV comedy *Arrested Development*, has made the show's first season available on Hulu. The network's top-rated reality show, *American Idol*, isn't available on Hulu at all. Fans of ABC's drama *Lost* have access to the show's first four seasons, but only part of the show's final last season. Hulu's inventory is made up of what the networks want to provide. This has been frustrating for Hulu's audience. Fans of *Lost*, for example, can watch most of the series, but won't be able to see how it ends.

In an interview for *FastCompany*, Will Richmond, a veteran analyst with Video-Nuze, a website and newsletter that covers news and analysis of the online/ mobile video industries, said, "Hulu was a breakthrough service, but people are never satisfied." He went on to explain that the online video-streaming environment was "a desert and Hulu provided water, but now the people also

Many of the top-rated shows on network television, including *American Idol*, aren't available on Hulu, which frustrated both Kilar and his viewers.

want food and table settings. On the web, people are accustomed to access, and they don't take kindly to restrictions."

Kilar is sympathetic to Hulu's viewers and the frustrations of incomplete content. "Users deserve to have whatever they want to watch," he told *FastCompany*. With the Hulu team, Kilar did his best to manage viewers' expectations. He was as clear as possible about expiration dates for shows and how long certain shows would be available. Hulu now posts expiration dates on episodes and it actively sends out e-mail alerts to registered users about what is available on its site.

CHAPTER 6

Kilar's Career After Hulu

Jason Kilar did a spectacular job running things at Hulu, and changed how viewers access and watch video content online. However, at times Kilar clashed with Hulu's owners on the company's strategy. Hulu's original owners, NBC Universal and News Corp., along with Disney, which joined the company in April 2009, struggled to decide on the company's direction. When Comcast, a large media and cable corporation, bought NBC Universal in January 2011, it was decided that NBC would become a silent partner in Hulu to avoid a conflict of interest. Kilar lost the vocal support of Jeff Zucker, then-president of NBC Universal and a key partner in promoting Kilar's ideas for Hulu. Zucker backed many of Kilar's ideas, including his advertising plan. When advertising sales executives at Fox and NBC complained that they were now competing with Hulu for advertisers to buy spots on their own networks' websites, Zucker told executives that there was enough space for all

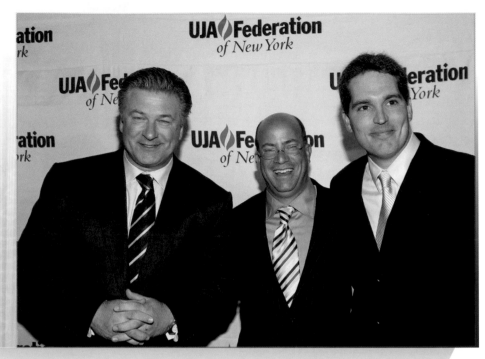

Actor Alec Baldwin; Jeff Zucker, president and CEO of NBC Universal; and Jason Kilar, then-CEO of Hulu, attend an awards reception in support of NBC's silent partnership with Hulu.

of them to work with the same advertisers. In an October 11, 2012, article in *FastCompany*, Zucker talked about Kilar's ability to manage competing demands: "I always thought Jason was very even-keeled about the fact that he had to deal with three media companies and one private-equity firm. I think he learned a lot of diplomacy in the process." Zucker praised Kilar in the same *FastCompany* article, saying, "Hulu is everything we hoped it would be but were never really sure it could be. It's almost shocking how successful the company has been."

Many television analysts point to Zucker's departure as the beginning of the end of Kilar's time at Hulu. A friend of Kilar's, who asked to stay anonymous, spoke to *FastCompany* and said it was only a matter of time before Kilar found his job to be too compromised by changes in Hulu's owners.

KILAR ANGERS CORPORATE OWNERS

Another turning point for Kilar was a blog post he published on the Hulu website on February 4, 2011. It was shortly after the announcement of the sale of NBC Universal to Comcast. The blog post began with an announcement. He explained that after a long negotiation period, television stations and shows produced by Viacom Inc., such as MTV, Spike TV, and two popular shows from the Comedy Central network, *The Daily Show with Jon Stewart* and *The Colbert Report*, would be available once again on Hulu. The agreement also meant additional content. Hulu viewers would get up to two-thousand episodes of numerous shows, from several networks owned by Viacom.

Kilar also decided to use the blog post to share thoughts the Hulu team had on the future of TV. He wrote that while distributors like the big four television networks and cable television would still play a role in the future delivery of television content, they would not be alone. "We believe that three potent forces will be far more powerful in shaping that future: consumers, advertisers,

Rupert Murdoch, CEO of Fox/News Corporation, was among those who complained that Hulu's advertising caused competition between Hulu and its corporate partners.

and content owners," he said. He pointed to complaints and criticisms consumers had been expressing about television viewing experience. He added the following:

> *"What we've heard:*
> *• Traditional TV has too many ads. Users have demonstrated that they will go to great lengths to avoid the advertising load that traditional TV places upon them. Setting aside sports and other live event programming, consumers are increasingly moving to on-demand viewing, in part because of the lighter*

ad load (achieved via ad-skipping DVRs, traditional video on demand systems, and/or online viewing).

• Consumers want TV to be more convenient for them. People want programs to start at a time that is convenient for their schedules, not at a time dictated to them. Consumption of original TV episodes will eventually mirror theatrical movie attendance: big opening Friday nights, but more consumption will be in the days and weeks afterward. Consumers also want the freedom to be able to watch TV on whatever screen is most convenient for them, be it a smartphone, a tablet, a PC, or, yes, a TV.

• Consumers are demonstrating that they are the greatest marketing force a good television show or movie could ever have, given the powerful social media tools at consumers' disposal. Consumers now also have the power to immediately tank a bad series, given how fast and broad consumer sentiment is disseminated. This is nothing short of a game-changer for content creators, owners, and distributors.

The above trends are a reality and we believe the wise move is to find ways to exploit these new trends and leverage them to build great businesses… It is clear to us that— because of the Internet and the increased competition/

innovation it brings—the future of TV is going to be very good to users, advertisers and content owners/creators."

At the end of his blog, Kilar wrapped up his dissection of the television industry by saying he hoped Hulu and his team could further change in how the industry works:

"*A number of you that are reading this might be thinking that we'd have to be crazy to think that our small team can actually re-invent television and compete effectively against a landscape of distribution giants like cable companies, satellite companies, and huge online companies. We are crazy. All entrepreneurs need to be. If it was easy, everyone would be doing it and there would be no naysayers. We are nothing if not a team that believes in the value of convictions, thoughtful stubbornness, and the relentless pursuit of better ways.*"

Many in the television and media industry agreed that the blog was both well written and a smart assessment of the current television industry. However, many also wondered what Kilar may have been thinking. Peter Kafka at AllThingsD.com, which published an article on February 3, 2011, about the blog post, outright asked the question, "Is Hulu's CEO trying to get pushed out the door?" As Kafka's article pointed out, Kilar was outwardly criticizing the three networks that owned Hulu and the many other networks and companies who were partners of the site. Kafka continued, "It's a lengthy read about the TV business and where it's headed, and most people I've talked to today think it's smart and well-written. Some of them also believe Kilar wrote it so that his bosses—executives at News Corp.'s Fox, Disney's ABC, and Comcast's NBCU—will give him the hook."

The blog post created waves for Kilar, with two of Hulu's owners making public comments about the post. Disney released a statement saying that Kilar's views were "personal and clearly not shared by anyone at Walt Disney." An executive at one of the other networks that owns Hulu, who asked to be anonymous, told Kafka that "80, 90 percent of what (Kilar) says is right. But why print that? Does he think we're going to say, 'Oh, thank you! You're right! We'd never thought of that! I can't see what he thinks will happen." In a February 2011 article in *Business Insider*, a person inside of Hulu, who also asked to be anonymous, said the company's owners were furious with Kilar and said, "If I were given billions of dollars worth of programming, I, too, could probably build a business....But I know that in order to build a long-term, viable business I would have to do so in a way that works for everybody."

Kilar never addressed the criticism publically, but according to several industry insiders who spoke with journalists at both AllThingsD.com and *Business Insider*, he privately reached out to his bosses at NBC Universal/Comcast, ABC/Disney, and News Corp. He also talked to

Hulu's numerous content providers, to offer an apology for bringing negative and unwanted attention to Hulu. Even though he apologized, his blog post created a rift in his relationship with Hulu's owners.

LEAKED MEMO SUGGESTS NEW DIRECTION, WITHOUT KILAR

In July 2012, a three-page, confidential, internal memo written by Hulu's corporate bosses was leaked to the public. The letter outlined several sensitive issues pertaining to Hulu and its future business plans. It also included one bullet point that raised the question of Jason Kilar's future with the company. The bullet read: "Outline transition plan for new CEO. Discuss potential candidates and process."

Kilar's future with the company had been the subject of speculation for nearly two years. Two of Hulu's owners, News Corp. and Disney, issued a statement after the release of the memo that supported Kilar. The statement said, "Jason is an outstanding CEO, leading Hulu to exceed our expectations while also uniquely positioning the company for ongoing growth in the long run. We look forward to Jason and Hulu continuing to expand Hulu's reach and deliver increasing value in the future." But the memo and the company's plan was out there. Many people saw it as the beginning of the end for Kilar.

According to the *Wall Street Journal*, in December 2012, Kilar approached his bosses to ask for more than $200 mil-

In January 2013, with viewership in decline and content becoming harder and harder to secure, Kilar announced his plans to step down from Hulu and pursue other interests.

lion to be used for acquiring more content for the site and expand Hulu's reach around the world. According to the article, there were—and are still—some competing agendas among Hulu's owners. The *Wall Street Journal* reported that sources at News Corp. said they want to see Hulu transition into a subscription-only service and leave behind its advertising plan. Sources at Disney reported that they want to see the company become a free service supported by advertising. These opposing views conflict with the direction Kilar had taken Hulu since 2007. Kilar never got an answer to his request for money.

A few weeks later, on January 4, 2013, Kilar announced his resignation from Hulu. In an e-mail that followed his announcement at a meeting with his staff, Kilar wrote, "For me, the journey started with a move to California and a walk into an empty office suite in early July 2007. In the weeks afterward, some brave souls that were willing to look past the many naysayers and jumped aboard and got about the business of innovating and building. Five and a half years later, thanks to the missionary work of this amazing 600+ worldwide team and courageous, prescient partners, we are fortunate to have collectively built a culture that matters, a brand that matters, a business that matters."

After Kilar's announcement, two of Hulu's corporate executives released statements about Kilar and his success at Hulu.

The Future of Hulu Without Kilar

In October 2013, Mike Hopkins, the former head of distribution for Fox, took over as chief executive officer of Hulu, filling the job nearly ten months after Kilar left the company. Many telelvision analysts say Hopkins has a big job ahead of him as he works to refocus the company Kilar shaped. According to an article in *Variety*, published in October 2013, the future of Hulu depends on a few factors, among them:

(continued on the next page)

Mike Hopkins, formerly a Fox executive, took Kilar's position and has the task of refocusing the company.

(continued from the previous page)

Get Hulu's Owners to Agree

Hulu's executives answer to three bosses and all three have different views of what the company should be doing. For Hulu to survive, the company needs to settle on one strategy and make it work. These are the main two directions its current owners want to go in, but they need to select one.

Challenge Netflix

One route is for Hulu to take on Netflix directly. If it establishes exclusive rights to top television and film content, it can create a sense that Hulu is the place to go for certain shows and films. Netflix is spending a considerable amount of money on securing content. If Hulu wants to compete and not lose its position to up-and-coming sites, it needs to begin buying content at a much quicker pace.

Do Original Programming

If Hulu is going to produce original programming, it needs to do it right by developing series that people want to see. Netflix's *House of Cards* and *Orange Is the New Black* are top-tier shows with big-name talent that have gone on to earn Emmy and Golden Globe nominations. If Hulu wants to be in this arena, it needs to commit or avoid it altogether.

"Jason has been an integral part of the Hulu story, transforming it from an interesting idea into an innovative business model that continues to evolve. We are proud of his achievements, we appreciate what he's built, and we share his confidence in his team's ability to drive Hulu forward from here," said Disney CEO Bob Iger in a statement released to the *Huffington Post* in January 2013.

News Corp. CEO Rupert Murdoch also released a statement that read: "Jason and his team have done a great job building Hulu into one of the leading online video services available today and it's incredibly well positioned for the road ahead. We are grateful for Jason's leadership and wish him the best on his next venture." Murdoch's statement also appeared in the *Huffington Post* in January 2013.

In his announcement, Kilar also thanked his team of coworkers, expressing his appreciation for their dedication to Hulu. But neither in his blog, nor during his personal announcement to his staff did Kilar give a reason for his resignation. In his final months on the job, Kilar set about creating a transition plan for his departure.

KILAR'S NEXT VENTURE

After Kilar left Hulu he joined the board of directors for DreamWorks. DreamWorks is the production company and film studio behind top-grossing animated films like *Kung Fu*

Panda, the *Shrek* trilogy, and *Madagascar*. He also launched his next initiative, the Freemont Project.

For the first several months, there was no information about the Freemont Project other than it was a secretive, consumer-focused venture. On the Freemont Project website, a short description offered the only clue to what that venture might be. The site's homepage reads: "*The Fremont Project* is the code name for a new consumer-focused venture founded by Jason Kilar (Founding CEO of Hulu and former Senior Vice President at Amazon) and Richard Tom (Former CTO of Hulu). We are based in San Francisco, California, and are hard at work on an ambitious mission. We are seeking innovators that pursue better ways in all that they do." The site was actively hiring software developers, software designers, and web developers. The name "Freemont" has personal meaning for Kilar and his business partner, Richard Tom. In an e-mail to *GeekWire*, Richard said, "The code name is a nod to a fun neighborhood in Seattle that Jason and I were very fond of."

After Kilar and Tom posted their hiring message, Kilar rented office space in Los Angeles, California, and began the interviewing and hiring process. Leading industry insiders, including several at *AdAge*, a magazine that follows media, technology, and the advertising business, thought the company would center on mobile media and video. Adding to the excitement was the fact that

There has been no formal announcement of the goals for Kilar's next venture, the Freemont Project.

several Hulu employees left to work for the Freemont Project. Kilar had already got Tom on board. Next came Loon Lee, Hulu's product vice president, and Megan Healey, Hulu's head of recruiting.

As of January 2014, Kilar still had made no formal announcement about the Freemont Project. He did, however, begin approaching several big publishers about his business idea. It seems to be similar in concept to Hulu, except that it focuses on written content instead of video content. According to a January 2014 article in *Re/code*, an independent technology news site, the speculation is that Kilar wants to create "an app that offers a collection of premium magazine and newspaper content, along with digital extras like videos, and lets readers pick and choose the stuff they want." According to the *Re/code* article, at least one publisher who met with Kilar about the idea said, "I love that a really smart guy is trying to do something innovative with premium content.... That's really cool."

Jason Kilar

Birth Place: Murrysville, Pennsylvania

Birth Date: April 26, 1971

Family: Father, Lance, an engineer for Westinghouse Electric Company; Mother: Maureen, humor columnist for *Penn-Franklin News* (Murrysville, PA); Siblings: brothers James, Jeffrey, and Kenneth; sisters Katie and Kerry.

Colleges Attended: University of North Carolina at Chapel Hill, majored in business and mass communications/journalism; Harvard Business School, Master of Business Administration degree.

First Job: Walt Disney Company, Disney Design & Development Department

Current Residence: Greater Los Angeles, California, area

Marital Status: Married to Jamie Kilar

Children: Four children

Net Worth: No published information available

Most Prominent Career Achievements Pre-Hulu: Became vice president and general manager of Amazon's North American media businesses; later served as senior vice president, Worldwide Application Software.

Hulu Career Achievements: Launched Hulu in 2008 as its founding chief executive officer; November 2009, Kilar negotiates with music companies to stream a variety of music events via Hulu; by 2010, Hulu announces that it could top $100 million in revenue by summer; by August 2012, Hulu has more than twelve million viewers.

HULU

2007: The idea for Hulu is generated between executives at NBC Universal, News Corp., and Providence Equity Partners, a private equity firm, as an online video joint venture; Jason Kilar is hired as Hulu's founding chief executive officer.

2008: Hulu is launched publically after a short beta testing period when users provided feedback on their experience.

2009: Disney announces that it will join Hulu and become a partner in providing content; Comcast buys NBC Universal. NBC Universal becomes a silent partner in Hulu to avoid a conflict of interest.

2010: Hulu launches Hulu Plus, a subscription-based service that provides viewers with high-definition content from a larger number of content providers.

2011: (January) Comcast merges with NBC Universal, which changes the ownership structure of Hulu. NBC Universal is now a silent partner in the Hulu business; Hulu earns more than $420 million in revenue; (October) Hulu announces a five-year deal with the CW network. The deal gives Hulu access to next-day content from five of the six major networks.

2012: Hulu debuts its first original scripted comedy, *Battleground*; Providence Equity Partners sells its stake in Hulu and is no longer an owner; Hulu generates $700 million in revenue.

2013: (February) Jason Kilar steps down as chief executive officer; (October): Mike Hopkins is announced as Hulu's new chief executive officer; Hulu reports more than five million subscribers to Hulu Plus.

2014: Hulu reports more than one thousand brands advertising on its site.

Timeline

1971: Kilar is born on April 26, in Pittsburgh, Pennsylvania.

1980: The Kilar family goes to Walt Disney World in Orlando, Florida. The experience begins a long fascination for Kilar with Walt Disney.

1988: The Kilar family moves to Boca Raton, Florida, during Kilar's junior year of high school.

1993: Kilar graduates from the University of North Carolina at Chapel Hill with a bachelor's degree in business administration and journalism and mass communication; works as a production assistant on a movie, *The River Wild*; joins the Walt Disney Company's Disney Development Corporation as an analyst for strategy and marketing.

1995: Leaves Walt Disney.

1997: Graduates from Harvard Business School with a Master of Business Administration (MBA) degree; joins Amazon as a product manager.

2001: Becomes Vice President first of Marketplace, and then of Books, Music, and Video & DVD. Is promoted to General Manager of North American Media for Amazon.

2002: Becomes senior vice president Worldwide for Amazon's Application Software division.

Timeline (continued)

2006: Kilar leaves Amazon and spends a year traveling the world with his wife and children.

2007: Appointed as the founding chief executive officer of Hulu.

2008: Hulu is launched to the public after a beta testing phase when feedback is gathered from users.

2009: *Entrepreneur* magazine names Kilar to its list of 25 Innovators in Technology for his vision and innovative use of technology in establishing Hulu as a leading video content provider.

2011: Kilar writes a blog post about the future of television in which he criticizes networks. Hulu's bosses at NBC Universal, ABC/Disney, and News Corp. are angered.

2013: Kilar steps down from Hulu and takes some time off.

2014: Kilar announces the Freemont Project, a media company designed to make magazine and newspaper content available online on a wider, more user-friendly scale.

Glossary

analog A mechanism in which data is represented by continuously variable physical quantities.

antenna A device (such as a wire or a metal rod) for sending or receiving radio or television signals.

app Short for application, the software that enables a computer to perform certain tasks.

blog A website on which someone writes about personal opinions, activities, and experiences.

board of directors A body of elected or appointed members that jointly oversee the activities of a company or organization.

brand A category of products that are all made by a particular company and all have a particular name.

cloud The computers and connections that support cloud computing.

commercial Paid advertising messages in newspapers, magazines, flyers, billboards, and paid announcements over radio and television to sell a product, item, or service.

concept An idea of what something is or how it works.

confidential Secret or private.

consumer A person who buys goods and services.

copyright The legal right to be the only one to reproduce, publish, and sell a film, musical recording, etc., for a certain period of time.

criticism The act of expressing disapproval and of noting the problems or faults of a person or thing.

demographics Statistics of a given population. Demographics are also used to identify the study of quantifiable subsets within a given population, which characterize that population at a specific point in time.

digital Relating to information that is stored in the form of the numbers 0 and 1.

docuseries A television series shot in documentary style.

equity A share of a company's stock.

hybrid Something that is formed by combining two or more things.

innovation The act or process of introducing new ideas, devices, or methods.

licensing A grant by the holder of a copyright or patent to another of any of the rights embodied in the copyright or patent short of an assignment of all rights.

medium A channel or system of communication, information, or entertainment.

memo A usually brief written message from one person or department in an organization, company, etc., to another.

mission A pre-established and often self-imposed objective or purpose.

navigate To make one's way over or through.

piracy The act of illegally copying someone's product or invention without permission.

planned community Any community that was carefully planned from its inception and is typically constructed in a previously undeveloped area.

resignation An act of giving up a job or position in a formal or official way.

revolutionary Causing or relating to a great or complete change.

sitcom A show that is on television regularly and is about a group of characters who are involved in different funny situations.

television network A telecommunications network for the distribution of television program content.

venture To start to do something new or different that usually involves risk.

vision A thought, concept, or object formed by the imagination.

webcast A transmission of sound and images via the Internet.

For More Information

American Public Media
480 Cedar Street
St. Paul, MN 55101
(800) 562-8440
Website: http://www.http://americanpublicmedia
     .publicradio.org
American Public Media is the largest owner and
     operator of public radio stations and a premier
     producer and distributor of public radio program-
     ming in the nation.

Canadian Broadcasting Association
P.O. Box 3220
Station C
Ottawa, ON K1Y 1E4
Canada
(866) 306-4636
This is a national public broadcaster and one of
     Canada's largest cultural institutions. It offers
     regionally and culturally diverse programming by,
     for and about Canadians, in English and French
     across the country.

Center for Media Literacy
22837 Pacific Coast Highway, #472
Malibu, CA 90265
(310) 804-3985
Website: http://www.http://www.medialit.org
The Center for Media Literacy is an educational
    organization that provides leadership, public edu-
    cation, professional development and educational
    resources nationally and internationally.

Digital Promise
1731 Connecticut Avenue NW, 4th Floor
Washington, DC 20009
(202) 450-3675
Website: http://www.digitalpromise.org
Digital Promise supports comprehensive research
    and development to benefit lifelong learners and
    provide Americans with the knowledge and skills
    needed to compete in the global economy.

International Academy of Digital Arts and Science
22 West 21st Street, 7th Floor
New York, NY 10010
(212) 675.4890
Website: http://www.iadas.net
The International Academy of Digital Arts and
    Sciences was founded in 1998 to help drive the

creative, technical, and professional progress of the Internet and evolving forms of interactive media.

Internet Society
1775 Wiehle Avenue, Suite 201
Reston, VA 20190-5108
(703) 439-2120
Website: https://www.internetsociety.org
The Internet Society's purpose is to promote the open development, evolution, and use of the Internet for the benefit of all people throughout the world.

National Association for Media Literacy Education
10 Laurel Hill Drive
Cherry Hill, NJ 08003
(888)775-2652
Website: http://namle.net
NAMLE helps individuals of all ages develop the habits of inquiry and skills of expression that they need to be critical thinkers, effective communicators, and active citizens in today's world.

National Center for Accessible Media
Carl and Ruth Shapiro Family National Center for Accessible Media at WGBH (NCAM)
One Guest Street
Boston, MA 02135

(617) 300-3400

Website: http://ncam.wgbh.org

NCAM's mission is to expand access to present and future media for people with disabilities; to explore how existing access technologies may benefit other populations; to represent its constituents in industry, policy and legislative circles; and to provide access to educational and media technologies for special needs students.

National Center for Media Engagement

975 Observatory Drive

Madison, WI 53706

(866) 234-2016

Website: http://mediaengage.org

As the digital revolution rolls on, this remains a critical time for locally licensed public media. The NCME will lead stations and demonstrate relevance, impact and the ability to engage with their community leaders, organizations and various demographic groups to address local concerns and ensure healthy communities.

North American Broadcasters Association

P.O. Box 500, Station A

Toronto, ON M5W 1E6

Canada

Website: http://www.nabanet.com

NABA membership is unique among the world's broadcast unions as it includes a large representation of American, Canadian, and Mexican national television and radio broadcasters and major suppliers of products and services to the industry.

World Wide Web Consortium
(718) 260-9447
The World Wide Web Consortium (W3C) is an international community where member organizations work together to develop web standards.

WEBSITES

Because of the changing nature of Internet links, Rosen Publishing has developed an online list of websites related to the subject of this book. This site is updated regularly. Please use this link to access the list:

http://www.rosenlinks.com/IBIO/Hulu

For Further Reading

Allain, Rhett, and Peter Vesternacka. *National Geographic Angry Birds Furious Forces: The Physics at Play in the World's Most Popular Game.* Independence, KY: National Geographic, 2013.

Anniss, Matt. *How Does WiFi Work?* New York, NY: Gareth Stevens Library, 2014.

Brandt, Richard L. *The Google Guys: Inside the Brilliant Minds of Google Founders Larry Page and Sergey Brin.* New York, NY: Portfolio Trade, 2011.

Brandt, Richard L. *One Click: Jeff Bezos and the Rise of Amazon.com.* New York, NY: Portfolio Trade, 2012.

Brash, Nicholas: *The Technology Behind: The Internet.* Mankato, MN: Smart Apple Media, 2011.

Chmielewski, Gary T. *How Did That Get to My House? Internet.* Nampa, ID: Cherry Creek Publishing, 2013.

D'Epiro, Peter. *The Book of Firsts: 150 World-Changing People and Events from Caesar Augustus to the Internet.* Harpswell, ME: Anchor Publishing, 2010.

Hutchins, Amy. *What Happens at a TV Station?* Jefferson City, MO: Weekly Reader Early Learning, 2009.

Grinapol, Corinne. *Internet Biographies: Reed Hastings and Netflix.* New York, NY: Rosen Publishing Group, 2013.

Keating, Gina. *Netflixed: The Epic Battle for America's Eyeballs.* New York, NY: Portfolio Hardcover, 2012.

Landau, Jennifer. *Internet Biographies: Jeff Bezos and Amazon.* New York, NY: Rosen Publishing Group, 2012.

Lastukka, Alan, and Michael W. Dean. *YouTube: An Insider's Guide to Climbing the Charts.* Sebastopol, CA: O'Reilly Media, 2008.

Machajewski, Sarah. *Internet Biographies: Mark Pincus and Zynga.* New York, NY: Rosen Publishing Group, 2013.

Marcovitz, Hal. *Issues in the Digital Age: Online Gaming and Entertainment.* San Diego, CA: ReferencePoint Press, 2011.

Robinson, Mathew. *Cutting Edge Careers: Careers in Computer Gaming.* Portland, OR: ReadHowYouWant, 2012.

Robinson, Tom. *Jeff Bezos: Amazon.com Architect.* Minneapolis, MN: ABDO Publishing, 2009.

Sande, Warren, and Carter Sande. *Hello World! Computer Programming for Kids and Other Beginners.* Shelter Island, NY: Manning Publications, 2009.

Sammartino McPherson, Stephanie. *Sergey Brin and Larry Page: Founders of Google.* Minneapolis, MN: Twenty-First Century Books, 2010.

Swanson, Jennifer and Glen Mullaly. *How the Internet Works*. North Mankato, MN: Child's World Publishing, 2011.

Staley, Erin. *Internet Biographies: Nick Swinmurn, Tony Hsieh, and Zappos*. New York, NY: Rosen Publishing, 2013.

Stone, Brad. *The Everything Store: Jeff Bezos and the Age of Amazon*. New York, NY: Little, Brown and Company, 2013.

Teitelbaum, Michael. *Innovation in Entertainment: Television*. Nampa, ID: Cherry Creek Publishing, 2013.

Vescia, Monique. *Internet Biographies: David Karp and Tumblr*. New York, NY: Rosen Publishing Group, 2013.

Vogelstein, Fred. *Dogfight: How Apple and Google Went to War and Started a Revolution*. New York, NY: Sarah Crichton Books, 2013.

Wallenstein, Andrew. "5 Ways New CEO Mike Hopkins Can Save Hulu." October 18, 2013. Retrieved February 24, 2014 (http://variety.com/2013/digital/news/5-ways-new-ceo-mike-hopkins-can-save-hulu-1200735150)

Woog, Adam. *YouTube*. Chicago, IL: Norwood House Press, 2008.

Bibliography

Accenture. "Five Insights into Consumer's Online Video Viewing and Buying Habits." July 2013. Retrieved February 21, 2014 (http://www.accenture.com/us-en/outlook/Pages/outlook-online-2013-five-insights-into-consumers-online-video-viewing-buying-habits.aspx).

Barr, Merrill. "Television May (or May Not) Be Dying, But Viewership Is Definitely Being Tracked Wrong." November 26, 2013. Retrieved February 25, 2014 (http://www.forbes.com/sites/merrillbarr/2013/11/26/television-may-or-may-not-be-dying-but-viewership-is-definitely-being-tracked-wrong).

Boostin, Julia. "Who is Jason Kilar?" July 10, 2012. Retrieved February 5, 2014 (http://www.cnbc.com/id/48142229).

Bulles, Jeff. "35 Mind Numbing YouTube Facts, Figures and Statistics – Infographic." Retrieved February 12, 2014 (http://www.jeffbullas.com/2012/05/23/35-mind-numbing-youtube-facts-figures-and-statistics-infographic/#bEOgtGAb6fhL7YlZ.99).

Edwards, Jim. "TV Is Dying, and Here Are the Stats That Prove It." November 24, 2013. Retrieved February 20, 2014 (http://www.businessinsider.com/cord-cutters-and-the-death-of-tv-2013-11).

Engler, Craig. "TV Economics 101: Why You Can't Watch Every Show Online for Free." May 4, 2010 (http://boingboing.net/2010/05/04/tv-economics-101-why.html).

Fritz, Ben, and Alex Pham. "Not Just for Games."
    June 5, 2012. Retrieved February 25, 2014 (http://
    articles.latimes.com/2012/jun/05/business/la-fi
    -ct-e3-console-entertainment-20120605).

Hansell, Saul. "Why Hulu Succeeded as Other =Video
    Sites Failed." July 8, 2009. Retrieved =February 5,
    2014 (http://bits.blogs.nytimes=.com/2009/07/08/
    why-hulu-succeeded-as-other-video-sites-failed).

Holly, Russell. "Netflix vs. Hulu Plus: Who Best Fits
    Your Video Streaming Needs?" September 26, 2013.
    Retrieved February 5, 2014 (http://www.geek.com/
    mobilenetflix-vs-hulu-plus-video-streaming
    -1530507).

Hulu. "About Us." Retrieved February 11, 2014 (http://
    www.hulu.com/about).

James, Meg. "Hulu Expects Long Ride on Online Video
    Wave." Posted July 14, 2010. Retrieved February 3, 2014
    (http://articles.latimes.com/2010/jul/14/business/la-fi
    -ct-facetime-20100713).

"Jason Kilar." Retrieved February 3, 2014 (http://www
    .kenan-flagler.unc.edu/about/our-people/meet-our
    -alumni/jason-kilar).

Kafka, Peter. "Former Hulu Head Jason Kilar's Stealth
    Startup Pitches Magazine Publishers." January 30,
    2014. Retrieved February 12, 2014 (http://recode.
    net/2014/01/30/former-hulu-head-jason-kilars-stealth
    -startup pitches-magazinc=-publishers).

Kafka, Peter. "Is Jason Kilar Trying to Get Fired?" February 3, 2011. Retrieved February 20, 2014 (http://allthingsd.com/20110203/is-jason-kilar -trying-to-get-fired).

Kilar, Jason. "Flip-Flops at Work? Fine." August 15, 2009 Retrieved February 13, 2014 (http://www .nytimes.com/2009/08/16/jobs/16boss.html ?_r=0).

Kilar, Jason. "Some News to Share." January 4, 2013. Retrieved February 20, 2014 (http://blog.hulu.com/ 2013/01/04/some-news-to-share).

Kilar, Jason. "Stewart, Colbert, and Hulu's Thoughts About the Future of Television." February 2, 2011. Retrieved February 24, 2014 (http://blog.hulu.com/2011/02/ 02/stewart-colbert-and-hulus-thoughts-about-the -future-of-tv).

Laporte, Nicole. "Hulu Struggles to Survive the Influence of Its Parent Companies." November 2012. Retrieved February 3, 2014 (http://www.fastcompany.com/ 3001736/hulu-struggles-survive-influence-its-parent -companies-update).

Levin, Gary. "The Netflix Impact: How Many Use the Streaming Service." September 23, 2013. Retrieved February 19, 2014 (http://archive.wkyc.com/news /smartliving/article/315402/349/Study-shows-38-of -Americans-use-Netflix).

Nakashima, Ryan. "Jason Kilar, Hulu CEO, to Quit by March." January 4, 2013. Retrieved February 11, 2014 (http://www.huffingtonpost.com/2013/01/04/jason -kilar-hulu-ceo-quit_n_2411875.html).

Owen, Rob. "Murrysville Native at Hulu Changes How We Watch TV." April 4, 2012. Retrieved February 13, 2014 (http://www.post-gazette.com/ae/tv-radio/2012/ 04/04/Murrysville-native-at-Hulu-changes-how-we -watch-TV/stories/201204040194#ixzz2tDQWrZJm).

Roettgers, Janko. "Jason Kilar's secretive Fremont Project Nabs More Hulu Talent." November 8, 2013. Retrieved February 3, 2014 (http://gigaom.com/2013/ 11/08/jason-kilars-secretive-fremont-project-nabs -more-hulu-talent).

Salter, Chuck. "Can Hulu Save Traditional TV?" November 2009. Retrieved February 20, 2014 (http://www .fastcompany.com/1400882/can-hulu-save -traditional-tv).

Wallenstein, Andrew. "Hulu CEO Faces Big Changes." August 19, 2012. Retrieved February 20, 2014 (http:// variety.com/2012/digital/news/hulu-ceo-faces-big -changes-1118058038).

Waxman, Haley. "Hulu CEO Speaks About Motivation, Success." February 25, 2013. Retrieved February 11, 2014 (http://www.dailytarheel.com/article/2013/02/ hulu-ceo-speaks-about-motivation-success).

Index

ABOUT THE AUTHOR

Laura La Bella is the author of more than twenty-five non-fiction children's books, including *Digital and Information Literacy: Building Apps* and *Careers in Computer Technology: Web Developer*. La Bella is a marketing and communications professional at Rochester Institute of Technology. There, she manages publications, is involved in writing and editing web content, and seeks out ways to use the latest technologies to improve publishing processes. La Bella lives in Rochester, New York, with her husband and son.

PHOTO CREDITS